# flea market
## BABY

# flea market
## BABY

the abc's of decorating, collecting & gift giving

*barri leiner & marie moss*

stewart, tabori & chang
new york

Published in 2003 by
Stewart, Tabori & Chang
A Company of La Martinière Groupe
115 West 18th Street
New York, NY 10011

Export Sales to all countries except Canada, France,
and French-speaking Switzerland:
Thames and Hudson Ltd.
181A High Holborn
London WC1V 7QX
England

Canadian Distribution:
Canadian Manda Group
One Atlantic Avenue, Suite 105
Toronto, Ontario M6K 3E7
Canada

Library of Congress Cataloging-in-Publication Data
Leiner, Barri. Flea market baby : the abc's of decorating, collecting, and gift giving / Barri Leiner & Marie Moss.
p. cm. ISBN 1-58479-308-2 1. Nurseries–Decoration. 2. Children's paraphernalia–Collectors and collecting.
I. Moss, Marie. II. Title. NK2117.N87L45 2003 747.7'7–dc21 2003054211

The text of this book was composed in (Century Schoolbook, Freehand 521, and Memphis).

Printed in China
10 9 8 7 6 5 4 3 2 1
First Printing

*for*
*emma & maisy*

# CONTENTS

wherever we go
A little vintage
twosome bestowed
upon Barri
as a birthday
treat from Marie

Once upon a time there were two girls named Marie and Barri who had been friends for as long as they could remember. While they shared a passion for movies, fashion, and travel, their favorite adventures were those spent searching for one of a kind finds together at the flea market.

Their storybook friendship at the flea began with once a month trips to the Kane County fairgrounds in Illinois to look for "smalls" (sterling charms and vintage rickrack). These perfectly pocket-sized treasures suited their city-sized square footage and could easily be tucked away for admiring and gift giving.

Soon their now and again junking journeys became need to go *now* excursions with plans penciled in for almost every weekend. When not flea-ing, they could be found following neighbor-hood signs to tag sales or making their way to antique filled

towns and junk spots. It was somewhere along this (or that!) rural route that their craze for collecting turned into an incurable case of junk fever. What began as a hunt to find one of a kind gifts for family and friends quickly became an appreciation (ok, obsession) for all things old. Their homes were soon stocked to the brim with everything from monogrammed kitchen linens and floral wrought iron light fixtures to chippy farm tables and Sunday paintings. It was the well-worn, well-loved and often handmade appeal of these finds that gave the girls their inspiration and the resources for gift giving and decorating. In fact, when it came to shopping for most anything they always looked for something old before buying something new.

It was no surprise that this "philoso-flea" carried over into the lives and rooms of their little ones. When they were moms-to-be their

**Above left: Baby beads worn proudly by Barri's mom**

**Above right: Barri's fairy tale moment at City Park in New Orleans, 1968**

**Right: Barri's cuddly crib pal, Mr. Brown, has been hanging around since 1965.**

**Above: Barri is ready for her close-up at a New Jersey swimclub.**

searches for nursery wares turned up unimaginative furnishings so they decided to give their daughters' rooms a vintage advantage by adding some "baby talk" to their junking journeys. They headed off in search of handmade quilts, vintage wooden toys, storybooks, and furniture they could reinvent into nursery pieces. They magically turned a bead board pie safe into a changing table and a flower box into a diaper catchall. Vintage book illustrations, flash and greeting cards, even printed hankies were framed and hung while embroidered tea towels took their place as window treatments.

Above: Marie was "down the shore" for this seaside snap.

Left: A sunny souvenir from her first vacation

The girls were thrilled with their daughters' retro rooms and this fresh approach to reinventing old-fashioned finds for a new generation. Friends and family were also smitten, by the sweetly styled look the girls had created and began asking for tips

Marie's beaded bracelet went from hospital to hope chest.

Marie dishes out the favors at her backyard birthday party.

on their nursery know-how. So lists were made, markets mapped out, and soon the girls were sharing their notebooks full of notions with all of the townspeople!

One snowy season, the two girls bundled up their nursery notes, flea market photos, and retro resources with a plan to share their ideas with parents and children everywhere. They collected their favorite ideas for bringing up baby with showers of good wishes, instant heirlooms, and a hint of history and by autumn's colorful arrival, the girls were delighted to announce the birth of *Flea Market Baby*.

And so the two girls and *their* two girls lived happily ever after with their flea finds.

Above: Barri's daughter, Emma, at home in her flea-found dollhouse, 1998

Opposite page: It's baby talk at the flea for Barri and Marie.

**Maisy Moss takes a stand on the sand with all things vintage, 2002**

## THE END

# 1

## NURSERY SCHOOL

announcements

heirlooms

decorating details

keepsakes

Previous pages:
Welcome a
newborn home
with an old-time
greeting.

This page:
Saddle up to
vintage lamps—
a bright idea for
the nursery.

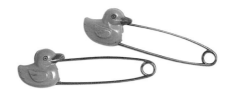

**welcome a little one** home to a nursery filled with the sweet simplicity of days gone by. From embroidered blankets and bedding to fresh-from-the-flea market furniture and fixtures, old-fashioned finds are the perfect way to feather a nest in one of a kind style.

Why not think of the flea market as your "retro registry" stocked with aisle after aisle of inspiration and endless decorating ideas. You'll want to rummage and sort through boxes and bins for textiles and trinkets that will help guide your vintage vision. Begin by scooping up tot-sized finds like pretty rolls of ribbon, patterned or printed fabrics, and whimsical storybooks. Tote home these treasures where you can use them as a guide for choosing paint palettes or playful decorative themes.

With a plan in place, set out in search of flea market furniture. Look to antique armoires for storage and waist-high cupboards that can easily be converted into baby's changing table. Keep an eye out for pint-sized pieces like children's chairs, tea party tables, and play kitchens to use as useful decorating details. With baby's bigger pieces in place, you'll want to set your sights on all of the extras, like frameable vintage book illustrations, cozy baby blankets and quilts, and old-time wooden playthings.

The abc's of nursery know-how begins with an eye for baby's basic needs layered with the sweetly styled notions of decades past. Swaddling a newborn in flea market style is the most comfortably clever way to raise baby the old-fashioned way.

MY NAME IS: ................................

.................................................................

I WAS BORN ON: ................................................

IN THE CITY AND STATE OF: .................................

MY HEART BELONGS TO MY DADDY: ...................

AND MY MOM: ...................................................

WITH A GENEROUS SLICE FOR MY FOLLOWING <sub>KISSIN'</sub> RELATIVES ............

Celebrate a little one's
arrival with baby
"booty" from the 1950s.
Favorite finds include
unsigned notes and
unused baby books with
retro graphics like this
*It's A Girl* book by
Helen Berry Moore.

# special delivery

**prepare to send** word of baby's arrival by setting out in search of vintage announcements. Whether you stumble upon a stack of mint condition cards or are inspired to design your own creation upon the find of a single graphic element, you're sure to delight friends and family with a good old-fashioned greeting.

Right: Don't pass up a one of its kind postcard announcement that can easily be color copied. The "Good News" is finding an unused box of beribboned cards.

Opposite page: Great gifts to polish up the nursery

ANNOUNCEMENT

MR. AND MRS.

ANNOUNCE THE ARRIVAL

ON

OUR
Good News

Every Flea Market
Baby deserves a
sterling start.
Silver wares, like
monogrammed cups
and rustic rattles,
are shining examples
of instant heirlooms.

# goodnight room

Got crib? Once you have picked out this store bought nursery necessity, give it a vintage vibe with layers of playful possibilities. Using the fun flea finds you've gathered as inspiration, begin to mix and match ideas for making baby's bed.

Create one of a kind baby bumpers with flea found fabrics like mattress ticking and feedsack florals. Why not double the fun by combining compatible prints and patterns for a two-sided treat?

*Oh sleep!*

*It is a gentle thing...*

*— Samuel Taylor Coleridge*

Handmade quilts are handy for bedecking a crib side while lightweight blankets are a stack up staple for snuggling. Tiny trimmings like pom-poms, patches, and rickrack can add a good old-fashioned finishing touch to simple store bought finds.

This page: A warm and wooly blanket for your funny bunny

Opposite page: A cute quilt and chippy chest of drawers give a new crib a vintage vibe.

**bead board baby**
Barri helped Marie hunt for this kitchen cupboard that was made "nursery new" with a fresh coat of paint, a cozy changing pad and a handy windowbox for storing diapers.

# *time for a change*

**topping any nursery** needs list is a changing table. Head to the flea with tape measure in hand in search of hip-height, flat-topped furniture like a chest of drawers, pie-safe, or farmhouse cupboard. All three of these alternative options to the traditional changing table can be outfitted with an easy to attach changing pad and offer built in storage. Even a vintage farmhouse table will work and can be dressed up with wall shelves above and baskets below.

**have fun collecting** vintage details that can deliver big style and a hint of history to every nook of the nursery. Once the furniture finds its place, you'll be set to add these easy extras. Find inspiration in items like a decal decked storage bin, a hometown hanky, a pottery planter turned lamp, or a collection of keepsake books. These do-it-yourself ideas will let you do up the nursery like a decorating pro.

retro ready
Left: A bucket
bears the load.
Opposite page:
Sweet as they
come second-hand
accessories

trunk show

**This page:**
**Feature fashion**
**too pretty to be**
**tucked away!**

**Opposite page:**
**A little lady-like**
**wool coat so**
**heavenly**
**handmade it**
**deserves to be**
**on display**

## window dressing

**get the nursery** all dolled up by wardrobing a window in homespun haberdashery. Doll clothes can be found in a bevy of prints and patterns sure to compliment any color palette and are as fun and affordable to find at the flea as they are for play. A ready-to-wear window treatment like this lets the sun shine in by day and can hide a black-out shade beneath to slip down for naps and night time. Even a just the right height coat rack can play host to an ever-changing fashion show of finds.

LUNCH

BABY

chair-y oh!
Pull up a chair for
baby's brunch
— just be sure it
meets modern-day
safety requirements
(ditto for all other flea
market baby finds).

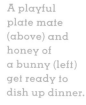

## happy meal

**serve your baby cakes** in cute cups and darling dishes destined to become family heirlooms. Look for bowls with wee-wonderful graphics, tin "baby" cups and little party-of-one extras like a Bakelite Scottie dog handled spoon and embroidered bunny bib. All are guaranteed to serve up the perfect vintage.

A playful plate mate (above) and honey of a bunny (left) get ready to dish up dinner.

*a cheerful look*
*makes a dish a feast*
*— George Herbert*

## cereal number

**This page:** Create a pint-sized place setting with plastic picnic ware, vintage linens and a jelly jar juice glass.

**Opposite page:** They'll eat themselves silly with this chow wow choo-choo.

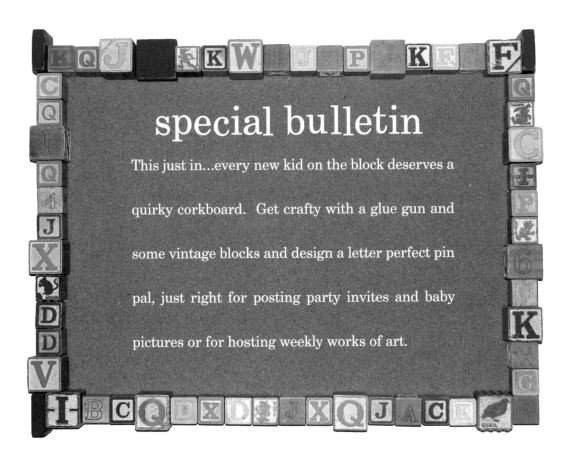

# special bulletin

This just in...every new kid on the block deserves a

quirky corkboard.  Get crafty with a glue gun and

some vintage blocks and design a letter perfect pin

pal, just right for posting party invites and baby

pictures or for hosting weekly works of art.

Opposite page: Mom, Kate Cohen, made this cork creation for her son Jack's room (she even hid secret codes and family initials in the design).

This page: A vintage wash bin stacks up as the perfect place to stow loved letters.

# book report

J IS FOR JAM   A IS FOR APPLE   Y IS FOR YARN

**one of the most** novel decorating ideas for baby's room is framing and hanging illustrations and images from pages past. Play the name game by framing the letter ready graphics of a vintage alphabet book to spell it out or picture an initial offering matted up to make a monogram. If breaking the book breaks your heart, create color copies or search fleas for on the loose pages ready for framing.

Above: A baby Jay would win the spelling bee with these framed pages from the *ABC Book*, Rand McNally & Co., 1958.

Opposite page: Ida is sure to bask under glass, a page from Charlotte Steiner's *ABC*, Franklin Watts Inc., 1946.

I

I for the island where Ida is staying

close knit

This page: Some
cuddly soft selections
from the flea

Opposite page:
Hand-painted hang-
ups from the 1940s

Johnson's
BABY
CREAM
Johnson-Johnson

# hanger appeal

**stock a little one's** layette with homespun hand-me-downs. Easy fit knits like cozy cardigans and cutie booties make nifty gifts and are perfect to pack for baby's ride home from the hospital. Best of all, you'll be dressing your wee one in instant heirlooms.

LITTLE BOY BLUE

# treasured chest

**the sweet souvenirs** of baby's beginning can be smartly stowed in a vintage doll trunk or small suitcase. Pack away tiny treasures like a hospital cap, first tee shirt, announcement, and greetings and you'll have created a three-dimensional scrapbook. As baby grows, toss in items like their favorite rattle, naptime blanket, and photographs. This tot-sized time capsule will encourage year after year of hands-on admiring of your kiddie's keepsakes.

super saver
Opposite page:
A few memory
making mementos
get tucked away
for tomorrow.

Right:
Case closed

# 2

# ROOM TO GROW

furniture

storage

collecting

clothes

Previous pages:
A bookend blondie
with a novel thought

This page: Cary takes
a seat at the Elephant's
Trunk Bazaar,
New Milford, CT.

Opposite page:
Scrappy Scotties
tell a tale.

**when your crib time cutie** is ready for a big kid bed, it's nice to know that most of the special nursery finds you decorated with will still make the grade. After you've swapped the crib for an iron bed or handsome headboard, take stock of the nursery pieces that can be reinvented into "big time" favorites.

Think about changing that flea market changing table into the perfect landscape for a vintage dollhouse or try filling the shelves with a series of hardcover chapter books or a child's souvenirs (let the gift of one snow globe snowball into a collection). Savor those first years by giving newborn keepsakes new jobs. Why not store crayons in a sterling baby cup or put extra bedding to rest in a little one's old bassinet basket? Even doll furniture, like a painted wooden wardrobe, can play a new role as nightstand or stand in as a gem of a jewelry box.

Whether you're starting from scratch or trying to please a first-grader's interior motives, adding a hint of vintage can be just the thing to give a room character. Keep an eye out for a storage ready armoire, create a cozy crafts corner with a chippy chair and table, and look for paintable partners like a dresser and dress up vanity mirror.

Scheming for a theme? Round up a few western wares like framed paint by number ponies and a cowboy hat collection and you've got a rodeo ready retreat or plant the seeds for a girlie garden room with flea market finds like Sunday flower paintings, tin toy watering cans and a bouquet of floral bedding. The best part of decorating with vintage finds is that most of them are destined to become treasured heirlooms.

*think big*

This page: Declare an open door policy for a perfectly packed armoire.

Opposite page (clockwise from left): A farmhouse hutch that was once a changing table makes a house call, an antique rocker takes a time out, and an able table tells a story.

like a house with good bones, hardy flea found furnishings
are sure to stand the test of time. While they will continue to endure
many more years of door slamming and drawer jamming, their ability
to adapt to any age will easily please even the most fickle little friend.

luau wow
**This girl's gone perfectly Polynesian.**

From that trusty chest of drawers to a vintage vanity, think of these special finds as investments in a child's furniture future. You won't believe how quickly the nursery armoire that helped you layout the layette can become your toddler's favorite "bookstore" or teen television "station."

tray chic
A shining
example of
sterling
accesories
and girlie
treasures

You'll teach a child's room to make the grown-up grade by adding extra credit items like wrought iron chandeliers, fancy framed mirrors, and sterling silver vanity accessories. These easy to add ideas get high marks for style and the decorating diploma for punching up a room's personality.

# hello dolly

**when not at play**, handmade doll dressers and cupboards from the 1940s and 1950s make swell stand-ins as side tables, nightstands, and sweet storage pieces. Slide a doll sized delight bedside and dress it up in the most unexpected way with an ever changing exhibit of toys and trinkets.

This page: A baby doll keeps watch over her decal-decked armoire in Sophie Rader's room.

Opposite page: It's a "good nite" for a good girl in Emma's room.

a stitch in time
Judy Hollenberg cross-stitched these samplers in 1965 for her niece (and our friend!), Rachel Rader. Today they can be found hanging bedside in Rachel's daughter Eliza's room.

# alphabet soup

The answer to personalizing a child's space is elementary. Simply spell it out with fashionably framed samplers or wood and metal letters from the flea market. Look for antique needlepoint designs or dig through bins of sewing notions for homemade hang-ables waiting to be turned into wonderful wall art. Collect single initials or gather a mismatched group to make a moniker—even clothes hangers can get the hang of it with glued on vintage game pieces.

**Above (clockwise from top left): "E's" up on the windowsill, Maisy gets hung up on fashion with a hanger designed by family pal and shopkeeper Nancy Laboz, and Emma Clary's moniker on a mantle.**

*Zzzzzzzzzzzzz*

**This page: "E"
is for Emma's
first big girl bed.**

**Opposite page:
Heavy metal
flea found beds
get comfortable
at home.**

# and so to bed

**when it's bedtime** for baby, tuck them into the sweet simplicity of an old-time iron bed. From a rounded rugged rig to a fancy *fleur de lis* frame, these sturdy sleepers are keepers. Make headway with headboards found in a room ready hue or paint a chippy find to match a mix of vintage bedding.

Ready to dress your iron maiden? Get girlie with feedsack florals, swirly matelasse coverlets, and hand-embroidered cases—the more prints for your princess the better. Or keep his camp campy with striped woolen blankets, plaid fringed throws, and ticking pillowcases. Now grab your favorite fairy tale, and turn out the light. Sweet dreams.

# stow
## away

**it can be as much fun** to stash, store, and stow your vintage loot as it is to find it in the first place. Think out of the toy box for some perfect put away ideas. Tidy up trinkets with a pocket perfect shoe bag, clip photos and cards to a lampshade for an everyday display, make a planter the perfect "post office," or send socks packing in a tie-front fabric envelope No need to keep kiddie clutter out of sight when it is totally neat-o!

**mess haul**
**Flea found hideouts
and hideaways for
keeping it all together**

61

## splish
## splash

**dip into ideas** for decorating a child's bathroom. Make big waves with little items like a monogrammed drinking glass, chenille bath mat, vintage tub toy, or silly soap dish. Kids will get in a lather over of these "just for me" flea finds and you'll soak up the compliments.

wash day
**Clean up at the flea with bath time bathing beauties.**

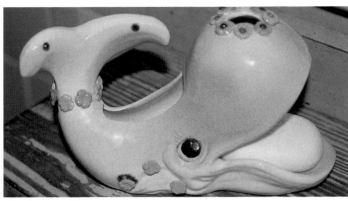

This page: A bead
board bookshelf revels
in all things rustic.

Opposite page: A
pet set of treasures

# collecting 101

**let a child's interests** and collections spark the decorating ideas. Discover retro room themes inspired by flea finds like signed baseballs, seashore sailboats, cabin keepsakes, and well-traveled souvenirs. You'll be creating *(continued page 69)*

**BOAT TOURS**

boy oh boy!
Shop for vintage nautical, western, and woodsy finds and you'll be saying, "I found it at the flea for my fella!"

DRINK Coca-Cola IN

# clothes call

**some of the most prized** Flea Market Baby finds are "new-old" clothing pieces moved from hope chest to hope chest without ever being worn along the way. From sweetly decorated sweaters and done up denim, handmade and old-time dime store wares are guaranteed to "wow" a child's wardrobe.

This page:
An in-jean-ious
find from our friend
Sandy Carlson

Opposite page:
(clockwise from top left):
Cute as a kitten cardi-
gans, walk-in-the-woods
wear, 1950s summer style,
and a trio of troopers

# 3

## PRESENTS WITH A PAST

parties

favors

gift wrap

vintage cards

Previous pages:
Ask a vintage
party pup cup to do
you a favor.

This page: Hats off to
"new old" birthday
stock found at the flea
for a (birthday) song.

Opposite page:
Offer them a piece of
cake from a delicious
birthday puzzle.

**plan a perfect party** by wrapping the theme around retro. Set a date for an old-fashioned at home, or backyard celebration, then begin the hunt for wonderful old party pleasers. Everything from unused invitations and fun favors to table and cake toppers can be gathered together to decorate and celebrate birthdays and baby showers in wow 'em with whimsy style.

You'll find inspiration in the good-time graphics of vintage party supply packaging. Take a hue cue from cutie items like candle boxes and candy cups or let "old school" illustrations be your guide when planning the particulars. Greet guests with penny candy treats and homemade eats that'll feed the vintage vibe.

Take best guest honors when the gift you give is a present from the past. Shower a friend with flea finds like a classic children's book of bedtime tales, a sterling cup, or a plaid woolen stroller blanket. Treat the birthday boy or girl to a vintage wooden puzzle, a stack of "new old" coloring books or some child-sized gardening gear. Wrap them all in vintage paper topped with an old-time trinket and get the party started.

# *birthday boy*

**when it's time to party** let your birthday boy's big day begin with a taste of tradition. Flea finds like place card poppers and party horns will fit right in with family favorites like a "best wishes" retro runner and little boy blue painted plate.

You'll keep guests guessing where you found the traditional treats when you fill goody bags with loot like pencil-by-number coloring cards, happy harmonicas, and decoder rings. Then invite them to the table to satisfy their sweet tooth with a delicious slice of the past.

**Flea markets are filled with age-old finds like packs of place cards, birthday buttons, and goody bag gear.**

76

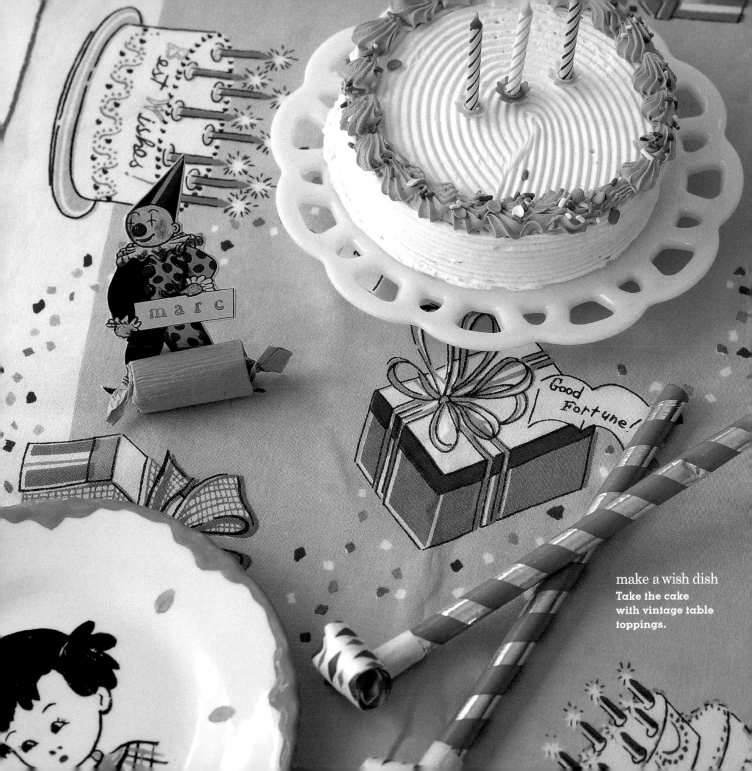

make a wish dish
**Take the cake with vintage table toppings.**

birthday suit
**Raise the
roof with a
retro
party plan.**

# party girl

**celebrate your sweetie's** big day with some old-fashioned fun. First whip up her favorite homemade cake or whisk away a decorated delight from the corner bakery. Give it stand-alone status atop a cake plate and bedeck it birthday style with a vintage toy destined to become the sweetest souvenir of the year.

**Set the soiree with nifty napkins, a birthday badge, and year-by-year candle.**

Treat the little ones to an afternoon of simple surprises like a retro round of musical chairs or a hide-and-seek scavenger hunt. Reward your good sports with flea found party pins and pastel paper goods and let them eat cake!

## goody goody

do guests a favor by handing out the treats and sweets of parties past (afterall, who wouldn't want a swell souvenir or two from a buddy's bash). They'll love a candy bar stocked with old favorites like gumdrops, wax pop bottles, and sour balls and will flip for goody bags stuffed with take home treasures like tiny tin trucks and dolled up dollies. **This page: Fashionable favors (above left) and a booty filled bonnet (right) Opposite page: Handy candy is served up sweetly.**

# how to be a wrap star

it's present perfect when you wrap it up vintage. Score a stack of pristine papers, retro ribbons and tie on toppers that will offer a happy hint at what's tucked inside. Go overboard for the birthday boy by wrapping a sailboat surprise in seashore style or play the numbers game by tying on a "two" for a smart little cookie. Think outside of the box with other toppers and stash a cache of cute gift garb like scalloped edge snapshots, counting cards, and mini doll accessories.

**Right: Good to go gifts get dressed in vintage.**

**Opposite page: Picture the possibilities.**

baby talk
**A mix and
match of
inviting ideas**

KATE

BABY

FOR
BABY'S
SHOWER

## great expectations set your sights on the stork's

**A 1950s stork does stand up for a crowd of cupcakes.** flight with a sweet celebration. Serve up the baby cakes, then shower mom with instant heirlooms like silver rattles, monogrammed cups, and engraved frames. Girlfriend guests will gush over the sentimental setting and delightful details.

# retro
# r.s.v.p.

Make a date to create vintage party invitations for a celebrating sweetie. Scour flea markets for a stunning stash of old stockroom-stored boxes filled with their never used notes or single stationary samples that can be color copied with the help of some hearty paper. Found a batch of cards without their envelopes? Treat them to a trip to the stationer to scoop up fun glassine or colored envelopes, retro-styled address labels, rubber stamps, and stickers. Feeling crafty? Deal yourself a perky picture card or choose an "age appropriate" game card to create any number of party possibilities. Now that's how to please your invitees!

maisy
is 1!

## paper parade

This page: Rescue a few boxes of old dime store greetings.

Opposite page (top to bottom): You'll get it write with an invite made on vintage paper (My Little Golden Stationery, 1951), and you can count on playtime playing cards.

# how old are you now?

**you can count** on vintage greeting cards for welcoming in the new year with memory making graphics and good wishes. Look for unsigned finds that send a special message for every year.

# 4

# PLAYING HOUSE

dollhouses

kitchens

dolls

Previous pages:
Dining in with
doll sized decals

This page:
A one-story
house

Opposite page:
Baby's boom box

THIS IS
MY HOUSE

A Chubby PLAYSKOOL Playboo

**from cooking up** a caper in a kitschy kid kitchen to making a house call to a handmade dollhouse, children will love playthings that play it up the old-fashioned way. Setting the scene (and the playroom) for days filled with make-believe moments will make a little one feel all grown-up while growing up!

The best thing about these pretend-with-me toys is that they make themselves right at home, in your home. A wooden kitchen heats things up as one of a kind room decor, a basket displays a collection of dishes like modern art and a grandpa-made doll-house joins a permanent room exhibit atop a table or bench.

You'll be amazed at the hours of fun and fantasy created by happy little house hunters making big decorating decisions. The recollection of your own collection will also delight you with these happy "homespun" treasures.

# home sweet home is what your child's

room will be when a handmade dollhouse moves in. Miniature moldings, art deco wallpapers and artsy architecture are just a few of the darling details that make these handcrafted homesteads hot properties.

In the market for a new house?

*There's no place like home.*

*— L. Frank Baum*

Be a retro realtor and comb the flea for the spare stylings of these made with love finds. Uncover a snowbound pink Shaker house, a shingled country cabin, an Austrian A-frame or a quaint Colonial and you'll have opened the door to an instant heirloom. Take stock of the stylish surprises left behind like faded country curtains, fancy floorboards, and fix-me-up furnishings, then tidy up the place and deck the halls and walls with an unexpected mix of dollhouse decorations.

Opposite page: Welcome to Maisy's Cape Cod with cutie curtains and shapely shutters.

97

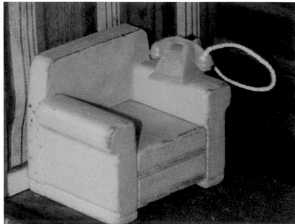

The Cape
Cod's
superior
interior

Items like tiny twin beds dressed up in checks and a table topped with itty-bitty dishes will keep the mix merry. Let scale pale and color scheme as you collect furniture of all sizes and hues, then fill in nooks with teeny treasures like handmade towels and cozy carpets. Daintily decorated? Now help a flea market family settle inside.

# room for rent

Sign the lease on a dollhouse made for storage. The soaring ceilings and sturdy structure of this sprawling second home offer the shelf help many moms dream about. Consider a bid on a handy hideaway like this where a kid-friendly floor plan can make housekeeping a happy chore.

**Two doll-lightfully filled floors of scenic storage**

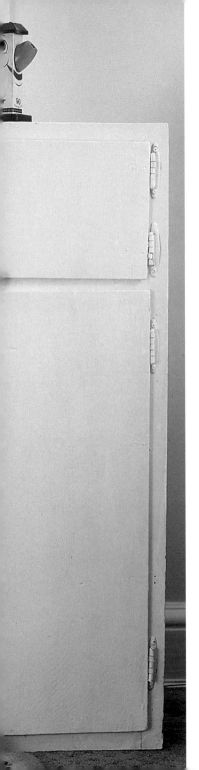

# *kitschy kitschy kitchen...*

## cook up a culinary corner

for a kitchen cutie with handmade appliances and homey wares. Little chefs will love a handcrafted kitchen complete with pull-open oven doors and slide-out silverware drawers stocked, and topped with canisters, cookbooks and flea market play food. The most delicious part of this playful playmate is the good taste it shows for fitting in with a bistro baby's furnishings.

Above and left:
Bake shop
bounty and
a tiny tin trio.

Opposite page:
Emma's kitchen
couture was an
Illinois flea market
find. Mom's recipe
for a fast fix-up
included glass
knobs and a new
baking dish sink.

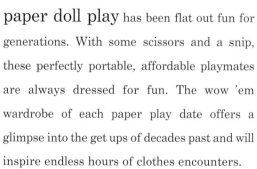

**paper doll play** has been flat out fun for generations. With some scissors and a snip, these perfectly portable, affordable playmates are always dressed for fun. The wow 'em wardrobe of each paper play date offers a glimpse into the get ups of decades past and will inspire endless hours of clothes encounters.

This ready-to-wear redhead was a scrapbook stowaway in clipped couture.

doll shop

This page:
Sweet fifteen
bisque buddies
from the
Grayslake
Antique Market
in Illinois.

Opposite page
(clockwise from top):
A vintage Vogue
wheelbarrow baby,
a huggable
Horsman honey,
and crepe paper
dressed partiers

# oh what
## a doll!

**surprise a little one** with a vintage baby doll. While modern mates may boast trendy tricks, these flea market filles and fellas inspire made at home make-believe magic.

Swaddle a cuddly cutie with labels like Vogue, Horsman or Effanbee and admire their molded hair, winking eyelids, and clever clothing, then arrange a nursery nook with a vintage cradle or crib, miniature quilts, and other sweetly-sized accessories.

It's a retro *runway* of made in Poland pals whose personalities are *punctuated* by their *hand-painted* faces and cute-as-pie clothing. Each posable persona *sports* a fashionable 'do, *along with* a head-to-

too take on the styles of their times. In *everything* from natty *nautical* wear to sporty aviator gear these little wooden wonders are *supermodel* souvenir right down to their *chic* little shoes.

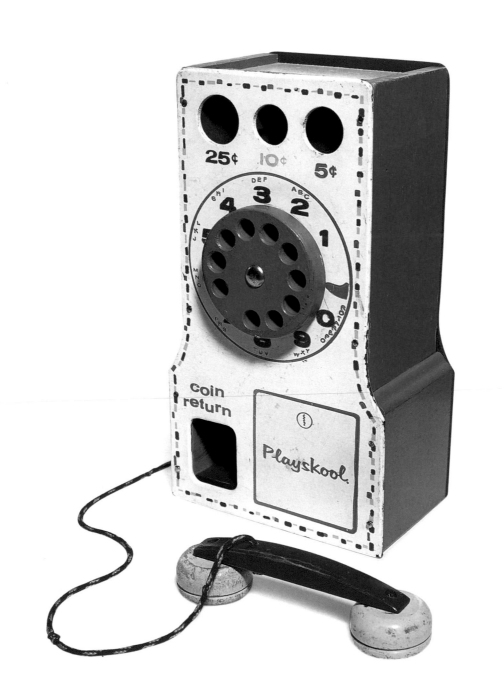

# 5

## TOY SHOP

wooden toys

puzzles

games

collectibles

Previous pages:
A clever coin
collector

This page: Pins of a
particular palette

Opposite page:
A topsy-turvy take
on spin art

TEN PINS

A "GOLD MEDAL" TOY

No 3145

MADE BY TRANSOGRAM CO. INC. NEW YORK.

RS INC.
LONDON

MADE IN
U.S.A.

make a play date with vintage toys guaranteed to fuel a child's imagination. These simply crafted creations are timeless treasures that foster fun for children of all ages.

From geometrically genius spinning tops and put'em-together puzzles, to steam-blowing metal trains and rainy day games, even the most modern mom will find a vintage toy story hard to resist. While the real treat of raising a child with vintage playthings is that these kiddy collectibles offer low-tech style with high impact, you'll also appreciate their humble and homey designs when they are left to roost out of their toy chest. And you'll love the retro reminiscing these toys can inspire and will soon see that by filling a playroom with them you'll be turning the space into a hope chest full of happiness for both you and your child.

Once you've set your flea sights on these vintage collectibles, you won't believe what's out there waiting to be rediscovered. Bins of building sets, wonderful wooden playthings, and crates of colorful puzzles are all so cute and clever you'll bring them home not only for their play time promise but for their ability to inspire decorating ideas and themes for a child's room.

mail call
**Sign, seal, and deliver first class fun with a playful Playskool mailbox.**

## *wood shop* wooden you just

love to treat your tot to a collection of old-fashioned playthings? Some of the best timber treats are primary painted pretend-with-me finds. Keep a keen eye out for a carryall case of colorful milk bottles and build 'em up blocks from memory-making manufacturers like Fisher Price, Playskool, and Holgate and you'll discover many of the same woody-wonders you played with as a kid.

This page: Playmates for parking permits (above) and a quite contrary dairy (right)

# going to pieces

THE THREE BEARS

GONG BELL
MADE IN U.S.A.

**it seems fitting** to tell an old-time tale, make a silly picture, or sharpen your state capitol skills with the perfect puzzle. Chunky wooden finds are handy helpers for smaller hands while cardboard-boxed sets will build a big kid's interest and imagination at every edge.

Flip over a two-story tell all from the Gong Bell Toy Company.

LITTLE LAMB

MARY HAD

## animal attraction

**little ones love** the cozy cuteness of a plush pet and often bond with favorites that offer them constant confidence and companionship. You'll find animal attraction among flea markets' furriest and will be particularly smitten with those creatures in need of a little care. Begin a vintage bear collection for your child, or make a rush for plush that boast hidden-inside music boxes for lullabies and good nights.

Opposite page: This tattered Teddy was a Paris flea market find.

Right: Maisy's mint mutt is musically inclined.

## after school special

**even a drizzle** can't fizzle the fun with flea market finds in the forecast. Make the most of fair or foul weather by stocking the shelves with stacks of old-time activities and clever crafts. Keep 'em in stitches with sewing cards, jump-start a junior journalist with a printing kit, or stage a costume party with pretty paper dolls all sure to make it a memorable game day.

art school
A bicycle basket built for supplies and a spicy solution for sparkling

winners circle
The goods to get
their game on.

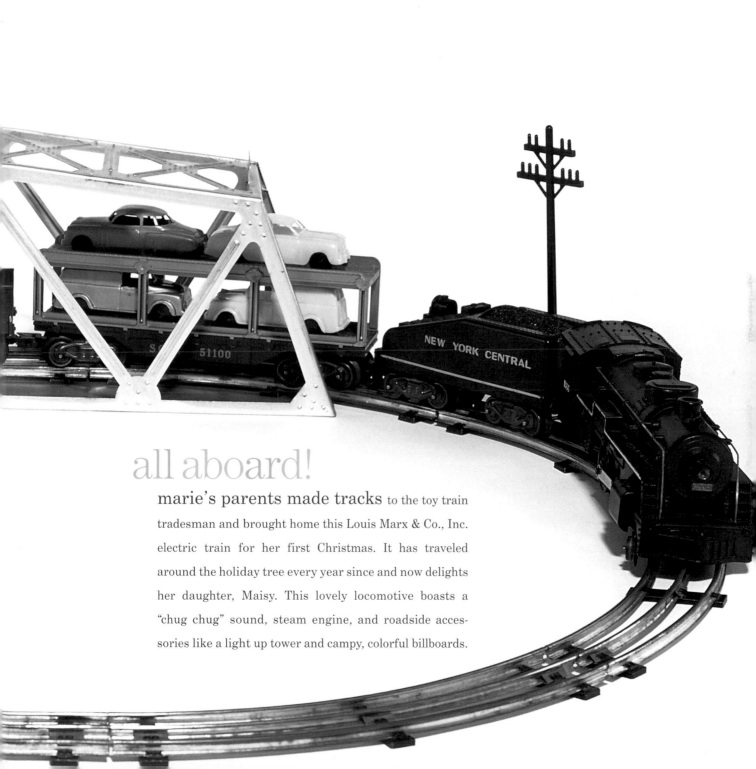

# all aboard!

**marie's parents made tracks** to the toy train tradesman and brought home this Louis Marx & Co., Inc. electric train for her first Christmas. It has traveled around the holiday tree every year since and now delights her daughter, Maisy. This lovely locomotive boasts a "chug chug" sound, steam engine, and roadside accessories like a light up tower and campy, colorful billboards.

# RETRO RESOURCES

## jump
### j

## old school
vintage furniture,
acessories, & clothing

**The Antique Center of
Red Bank**
195b, 195, & 226 W. Front
Street
Red Bank, NJ 07701
732.741.5331
732.842.3393
732.842.4336

**Antique Trove**
2020 N. Scottsdale Road
Scottsdale, AZ 85257
480.947.6074
www.antiquetrove.com

**Antique Centre**
2012 N. Scottsdale Road
Scottsdale, AZ 85257
480.675.9500

**Beverly's Collectibles**
902 Federal Road (Route 7)
Brookfield, CT 06804
203.255.0870

**Bittersweet Antiques**
Debby Gorin
37 Main Street
Tarrytown, NY 10591
914.366.6292
and by appointment

**Brooke James Ltd.**
773.252.4620
www.brookejames.com
by appointment

**Cottage Antiques**
1202 Route 35
South Salem, NY 10590
914.763.3773

**Hen House Antiques**
Rick and Linda Gibson
12721 Coleta Road
Sterling IL, 61081
815.622.0987
by appointment

**Heritage Trail Mall**
410 Ridge Road
Wilmette, IL 60091
htmltd@ameritech.net
847.256.6208

**Little Angel Creations**
Maria Amdur
29 Manchester Drive
Mt. Kisco, NY 10549
by appointment
914.242.4576

**Nancy Powers**
seller id: nancypowers
www.ebay.com

**Sage Antiques**
Susan Goldsweig
P.O. Box 134
Yonkers, NY 10710
914.912.3546
by appointment

**Vintage Home**
Rosanna Fiore-Tranzillo
144 King Street
Chappaqua, NY 10514
914.238.3014

## playroom
old toys & books

**Just Kids Nostalgia**
310 New York Avenue
Huntington, NY 11743
631.423.8449
www.justkidsnostalgia.com

**Old Well Antiques**
45 North Main Street
S. Norwalk, CT 06854
203.838.1842

**Scott Saltzman**
seller id: Scooter1z
scott.saltzman@verizon.net
www.ebay.com

**Toy Town of
New Jersey on ebay**
seller id:
toytownusaofnewjersey
www.ebay.com

**Uncle Fun**
1338 West Belmont
Chicago, IL 60657
773.477.8223
www.unclefunchicago.com

## general store
vintage & new
furniture, bedding,
clothing, toys, & gifts

**Always the Children**
27 S. Greeley Avenue
Chappaqua, NY 10514
914.238.7500

**Bu and the Duck**
106 Franklin Street
New York, NY 10013
212.431.9226
info@buandtheduck.com

**City Cricket**
215 W. 10th St.
New York, NY 10014
212.242.2258
www.citycricket.com

**E.A.T. Gifts**
1062 Madison Avenue
New York, NY 10028
212.861.2544

**Eliza Hugh**
Barbara E. Roetman
P.O. Box 644
99 Main Street
Lake Placid, NY 12946
773.525.4100

**Elizabeth Marie**
3612 N. Southport
Chicago, IL 60657
773.525.4100

**lmnop**
2574 N. Lincoln Avenue
Chicago, IL 60614
773.975.4055
www.lmnopkids.com

**Me & Ewe Company**
Meredith Cohen
105 Fifteenth Street
Wilmette, IL 60091
847.920.9290
www.meandewe.com

**Plain Jane Kids**
525 Amsterdam Avenue
New York, NY 10024
212.595.6916
www.plainjanekids.com

## skates
### sk

# dress
## dr

The Red Balloon
Company
2060 N. Damen Avenue
Chicago, IL 60647
773.489.9800
877.969.9800
www.theredballoon.com

Snippy's
1024 Third Avenue
New York, NY 10021
212.230.1300

Sundries
Betsy Goodman
701 N. Bedford Road
Bedford Hills, NY 10507
914.244.9020

Warm Biscuit
Bedding Co.
800.231.4231
www.warmbiscuit.com

## you're invited
paper & craft supplies

The Ink Pad
22 Eighth Avenue
New York, NY 10014
212.463.9876
www.theinkpadnyc.com

Kate's Paperie
www.katespaperie.com

Paper Source
www.paper-source.com

Parcel
Nancy Laboz
559 Bloomfield Avenue
Montclair, NJ 07042
973.744.7700
info@parcel.com

## to market to market
flea market, antique,
& collectible shows

Annex Antique Fair &
Flea Market
Avenue of the Americas
(between 24th & 26th
Streets)
New York City, NY 10011
212.243.5343
212.243.7922 day of market

Elkhorn Antique
Flea Market
411 East Center Street
Elkhorn, WI 53121
262.723.5651

Brimfield Antiques
& Collectibles Show
Route 20
Brimfield, MA 01010
413.245.3436
www.jandj-brimfield.com

Elephant's Trunk Bazaar
490 Danbury Road
New Milford, CT 06776
860.355.1448

The Garage Antiques
& Collectibles
112 W. 25th Street
(between Avenue of the
Americas & 7th Avenue)
New York, NY 10002
212.647.0707 or
212.463.0200

Grayslake Antique
& Collectibles Market
Lake County Fairgrounds
Route 120 & US45
Grayslake, IL 60130
715.526.9769
www.zurkoantique
tours.com

Kane County Antique
Flea Market
Kane County Fairgrounds
Route 64 & Randall Road
St. Charles, IL 60174
630.377.2252
www.kanecountyflea
market.com

Long Beach Outdoor
Antique & Collectible
Market
Long Beach
Veterans Stadium
Conant Street
between Lakewood Blvd
& Clark Avenue
Long Beach, CA 90808
323.655.5703
www.longbeachantique
market.com

# city
## c

# thread
## thr

Marche aux Puces
Porte de Vanves/Porte
Didot
Avenue Georges
Lafenestre/Avenue Marc
Sangnier
75014 Paris, France

The Pec Thing
Antique Market
Winnebago County
Fairgrounds
500 W. 1st Street
Pecatonica, IL 61063
800.238.3587
www.winnebagocounty
fair.com

Puces de St-Ouen
Porte de St-Ouen/Porte de
Clignancourt
75018 Paris, France

Rose Bowl Flea Market
Rose Bowl Stadium
Pasadena, CA 91103
323.560.show
www.rgcshows.com

Sandwich Antiques
Market
The Fairgrounds
State Route. 34
Sandwich IL 60548
773.227.4464
815.786.3337 day of show
www.antiquemarkets.com

Stormville Airport
Antique Show
& Flea Market
Route. 216
Stormville, NY 12582
845.221.6561

Wolff's Allstate Arena
Outdoor Flea Market
Rosemont, IL 60018
847.524.9590
www.wolffsfleamarket.com

## outta sites
websites & resources

www.ebay.com
online auction site

www.les-puces.com
French flea market site

www.whatsit
worthtoyou.com
online appraisals

# coat
## oa

**Gathering Moss at the beach**

# we're sweet on...

Our publisher, Leslie Stoker, whose vision has guided us from our very first steps. Our talented designer, art director and fellow Jersey girl, Nicole Salzano, for her friendship, patience, and hospitality. Beth Huseman for her way with words, and Kim Tyner, Caroline Enright, and the gang at STC for their steadfast support. Aimée Herring for her snazzy snaps and sweet sensibility, Thomas Mangieri for his help and humor and Marc Berenger at Lightbox Studio for letting the sun shine in. Rosanna Fiore-Tranzillo of Vintage Home for her welcoming ways and pretty props. Meredith Cohen of Me & Ewe Co. for her blanket statements. The Clary clan, retro Rader family and stylin' Saltzman's for playing house. Maria Amdur, Kate Cohen, Nancy Cohen, Katie Ginsberg, Beth Herbst, Nancy Laboz, Tracey Warshaw, and Dawn Yoselowitz for inspiring ideas and loaning the loot. Debby and Rosie for their caring ways.

The flea market babies—Marc and Ryan, Violet, Lucy, Emma, Bella and Charlie, Eliza, Sophie and Teddy, Mia, Kelsey and Jesse, Willie, Maddie and Mookie, Hanna and Chloe, Sam, Jack and Lucy.

Opposite page **(row one)**: Barri's mom, Ellen; **Marie's mom, Marie, and sister Frances;** B with her mom; M on a zoo date with **Mom and grandmother Emma;** B's husband, Eddie. **(row two):** B's dad, Neil; **Baby M;** M's Dad, Carl with Uncle Fritzi; **B with Dad and the ducks;** M with Mom and Dad. **(row three):** Danna sittin' pretty on sister B's lap; **B's brothers Matt and J in perfect harmony;** M and Mom in Miami; **Baby B;** M's great grandmother, Josephine and her grandmother, Josephine. **(row four):** B's grandpa Bernard; **B's grandmas Basch and Marge;** M's grandfather, Fritz, with her dad and uncle Bee Bee. **(row five):** M's husband, Stephen; **M's grandpop, Eddie, with her uncle Ronnie;** B's daughter Emma, a six-year-old trooper; **B with papa Gene;** M's one year-old Maisy.

Marie's mad about Maisy Hazel for making life a picnic. STM for being proud and always admiring the haul. Marianne for her sister-pal encouragement, love and giggles that go way back. Barri (my partner-in-rhyme!) for a friendship that can magically turn the everyday into a reason to celebrate. And Mom for Mary Poppins Sundays, backyard birthdays, boardwalks and always believing that dreams can come true.

To sweet Emma Jayne for cozy-quilt-nights and Moon Song snuggles, Mom for candy purses, beach days, and lovin' me a bushel-and-a-peck. Dad (Grampsy!) for Sundays in the park, NYC adventures, and the whole, wide world. Danna for camp songs and can you believe it. Matt and J., for the living room repertoire. Marie for a fairytale friendship a girl could only dream of and for being the reason in every rhyme, and Eddie, for all the happy endings. —xo, Barri

**B's family tree**